THE INDIAN VILLAGES

A STUDY OF THE CULTURE, TRADITIONS, AND WAY OF LIFE IN INDIAN VILLAGES

DR. JAGADEESH PILLAI

|| "Dedicated to all who seek to understand and
appreciate Indian culture and tradition." ||

Contents

Contents

PRAYER

**"Om Poornamadah Poornamidam Poornat
Poornamudachyate,Poornasya Poornamaadaya
Poornamevavashishyate,Om Shantih, Shantih, Shantih"**

*The literal interpretation of this mantra is: That which is
Absolute, This which is Absolute, Absolute arises from Absolute,
If Absolute is removed from Absolute, Absolute remains
OM Peace, Peace, Peace.*

ABOUT THE AUTHOR

Dr. Jagadeesh Pillai is a renowned Guinness World Record holder, writer, and researcher hailing from Varanasi, also known as the abode of Lord Shiva. With a Ph.D. in Vedic Science and a range of creative ideas and achievements, he is a true polymath. He is the author of more than 100 books including Research Publications. Although his roots can be traced back to Kerala, the people of Varanasi hold him in high regard and affectionately consider him one of their own.

Dr. Pillai has achieved four Guinness World Records in the following subjects:

"Script to Screen" - In this record, Dr. Pillai produced and directed an animation film within the shortest time possible, breaking the previous record set by Canadians. He has also received numerous national and international awards and recognitions for this achievement.

Longest Line of Postcards - For this record, Dr. Pillai created a line of 16,300 postcards on the occasion of the 163rd anniversary of Indian Postal Day. The event also included a questionnaire about the Indian flag.

Largest Poster Awareness Campaign - Dr. Pillai designed an awareness campaign on the subject of "Beti Bachao - Beti Padhao" (Save the Girl Child - Educate the Girl Child) to achieve this record.

Largest Envelope - In tribute to the Indian Prime Minister's

"Make in India" initiative, Dr. Pillai created a 4000 square meter envelope using waste paper to achieve this record.

Attempted - **70000 Candles on a 210 kg Cake** - To celebrate the 70th Indian Independence Day, Dr. Pillai attempted to light 70,000 candles on a 210 kg cake, which was recorded in World Records India.

Attempted - **Documentary on Dhamek Stupa of Sarnath in 17 Languages** - Dr. Pillai attempted to create a documentary on the Dhamek Stupa of Sarnath, dubbing it in 17 different languages. The result of this attempt is currently awaiting confirmation from the Guinness World Records.

Dr. Pillai is skilled in teaching the Bhagavad Gita, a Hindu scripture, and is popular among young people. He has helped many young people improve their lives through his motivational teachings.

In addition to teaching, he has composed and sung numerous Sanskrit Bhajans and patriotic songs.

He has also written and directed several short films and documentaries for awareness campaigns, and has volunteered with the police in both UP and Kerala to spread awareness about various issues through videos and photography.

Incredibly, he has produced and directed over 100 documentaries about the city of Varanasi, all on his own.

He has also helped and guided more than 25 boys and girls to achieve world records through creative and innovative methods. He is a multifaceted person who uses his intellect and the blessings given to him by God to excel in various areas. He is both a teacher and a student, always learning and teaching, and is able to master any subject he comes across.

He is a selfless social activist and motivational speaker who has overcome struggles and failures to become a successful and enthusiastic individual with a rich life experience.

In addition to his work with the Bhagavad Gita, he is also an efficient Tarot card reader, Astro-Vastu consultant, and a talented singer and composer. He has sung the entire Ram Charita Manas and Bhagavad Gita in his own compositions, and has sung the phrase "Lokah Samastha Sukhino Bhavantu" in 50 different languages. He is currently working on a detailed and scientific study of Vedas, Upanishads, Puranas, and the Bhagavad Gita. He has also composed and sung the Hanuman Chalisa and Gayatri Mantra in 108 and 1008 different compositions, respectively.

Awards - Four Times Guinness World Records, Winner of Mahatma Gandhi Vishwa Shanti Puraskar, Mahatma Gandhi Global Peace Ambassador, Kashi Ratna Award, Dr. APJ Abdul Kalam Motivational Person of the Year 2017, Mother Teresa Award, Indira Gandhi Priyadarshini Award, Bharat Vikas Ratna Award, Udyog Ratna Award, Vigyan Prasar Award, Poorvanchal Ratn Samman.

PREFACE

This book, "The Indian Villages: A Study of the Culture, Traditions, and way of Life in Indian Villages" aims to provide a comprehensive understanding of the culture, traditions, and way of life in Indian villages. India, being a diverse country, is home to a wide variety of cultures, traditions, and lifestyles. The Indian villages, in particular, are a reflection of this diversity and are an integral part of the country's cultural heritage.

The book is divided into 11 chapters, each of which explores a different aspect of village life in India. The first chapter, "Introduction: An overview of the importance of Indian villages in the country's cultural heritage and an examination of the challenges facing rural communities in modern India" provides a general overview of the significance of Indian villages in the country's cultural heritage and an examination of the challenges facing rural communities in modern India.

The second chapter, "The Culture of Indian Villages" delves deeper into the traditional customs, beliefs, and practices of Indian villages, including festivals, religious practices, and community life. The third chapter, "The Traditions of Indian Villages" explores the traditional art forms, crafts, and occupations of Indian villages, including pottery, weaving, and agriculture. The fourth chapter, "The Architecture of Indian Villages" examines the traditional architectural styles of Indian villages, including the use of mud, bamboo, and other natural materials.

The fifth chapter, "The Food and Cuisine of Indian Villages" explores the traditional food and cuisine of Indian villages, including the use of locally sourced ingredients and cooking techniques. The sixth chapter "The Education System of Indian Villages" examines the traditional education system of Indian villages and the challenges facing rural communities in terms of access to education. The seventh chapter "The Health System of Indian Villages" explores the traditional health system of Indian villages and the challenges facing rural communities in terms of access to healthcare.

The eighth chapter "The Role of Women in Indian Villages" examines the traditional roles and responsibilities of women in Indian villages and the challenges they face in modern society. The ninth chapter "The Role of Men in Indian Villages" examines the traditional roles and responsibilities of men in Indian villages and the challenges they face in modern society. The tenth chapter "The Challenges Facing Indian Villages" explores the challenges facing Indian villages in modern times, including poverty, lack of access to education and healthcare, and environmental degradation.

Finally, the eleventh chapter "The Future of Indian Villages" examines the efforts being made to preserve and promote the culture, traditions, and way of life of Indian villages, and the potential for sustainable development in rural communities.

This book is intended to provide a detailed and comprehensive understanding of the culture, traditions, and way of life in Indian villages. It aims to serve as a valuable resource for researchers, students, policymakers, and anyone interested in understanding the rich cultural heritage of India's rural communities.

I

Introduction: An overview of the importance of Indian villages

Introduction: An overview of the importance of Indian villages in the country's cultural heritage and an examination of the challenges facing rural communities in modern India.

Indian villages are an integral part of the country's cultural heritage. They represent the traditional way of life, customs, and beliefs of the Indian people and are a reflection of the country's rich cultural diversity. Indian villages are known for their simplicity, warmth, and strong community spirit. They are the backbone of the Indian economy and play a crucial role in preserving the country's cultural heritage.

However, despite their importance, Indian villages are facing several challenges in modern times. The rapid pace of urbanization and industrialization has led to a decline in the traditional way of life in villages. Many people have migrated to urban areas in search of better economic opportunities, leaving behind the elderly and children. This has led to a decline in the population of villages and a loss of traditional knowledge and skills.

Another major challenge facing Indian villages is poverty. Many villagers are living below the poverty line and do not have access to basic amenities such as education, healthcare, and sanitation. This has led to poor living conditions and a lack of opportunities for the villagers.

Environmental degradation is also a major challenge facing Indian villages. Overuse of natural resources, deforestation, and pollution have led to a decline in the quality of the environment and a loss of biodiversity. This has a negative impact on the livelihoods of villagers who depend on the environment for their survival.

Despite these challenges, there are efforts being made to preserve and promote the culture, traditions, and way of life of Indian villages. The government of India has implemented several schemes to provide financial assistance and support to villagers. Non-government organizations (NGOs) and private organizations are also working to promote and preserve Indian villages by organizing exhibitions, workshops, and training programs.

Indian villages are an integral part of the country's cultural heritage and play a crucial role in preserving the traditional way of life, customs, and beliefs of the Indian people. However, they are facing several challenges in modern times, including population decline, poverty, and environmental degradation. Despite these challenges, there are efforts being made to preserve and promote the culture, traditions, and way of life of Indian villages by the government and private organizations.

It is important to recognize the importance of Indian villages in the country's cultural heritage and to take steps to support and sustain them for future generations to come. This book aims to provide a deeper understanding of the culture, traditions, and way of life in Indian villages and the challenges they are facing in modern India.

*"The village is the epitome of Indian culture
and values" - Ashok Mitra*

II

The Culture of Indian Villages:

The Culture of Indian Villages: A study of the traditional customs, beliefs, and practices of Indian villages, including festivals, religious practices, and community life.

The Culture of Indian Villages: A study of the traditional customs, beliefs, and practices of Indian villages, including festivals, religious practices, and community life

The culture of Indian villages is a rich tapestry of traditional customs, beliefs, and practices that have been passed down through generations. These customs, beliefs, and practices are an integral part of the village life and shape the way of living, thinking, and behaving of the villagers.

One of the most important aspects of the culture of Indian

villages is the celebration of festivals. Villages in India have their own set of festivals that are celebrated with great enthusiasm and fervor. These festivals are an important part of the village's cultural heritage and bring together the entire community to celebrate and honor their traditions. Some of the most popular festivals celebrated in Indian villages include Diwali, Holi, Pongal, and Navaratri.

Religious practices also play a significant role in the culture of Indian villages. Villagers in India have a deep-rooted faith in their religion, and this is reflected in their daily lives. Many villagers participate in religious rituals and ceremonies, and there are a number of temples, shrines, and other religious places of worship in most villages.

Community life in Indian villages is also an important aspect of the culture. Villagers in India have a strong sense of community and are known for their hospitality and warm nature. They often come together to celebrate festivals and special occasions, and also help each other during difficult times. The village Panchayat (council) plays a vital role in maintaining the social order and solving the disputes and problems of the village.

The culture of Indian villages is a rich tapestry of traditional customs, beliefs, and practices that have been passed down through generations. Festivals, religious practices, and community life are an important part of the village culture and shape the way of living, thinking, and behaving of the villagers. This chapter will delve deeper into these aspects of the culture of Indian villages and explore the significance of these customs, beliefs and practices in the daily lives of the villagers.

"The village is the key to understanding India" - Mahatma Gandhi

III

The Traditions of Indian Village

The Traditions of Indian Villages: An exploration of the traditional art forms, crafts, and occupations of Indian villages, including pottery, weaving, and agriculture.

The traditions of Indian villages are an important aspect of the country's cultural heritage. These traditional art forms, crafts, and occupations have been passed down through generations and are an integral part of village life.

One of the most popular traditional art forms in Indian villages is pottery. Pottery is an ancient craft that has been practiced in India for centuries. Villagers use clay to make a wide variety of pottery items such as pots, bowls, and vases. The pottery made in Indian villages is known for its intricate designs and vibrant colors.

Weaving is another traditional craft that is widely practiced in Indian villages. Villagers use locally sourced materials such as cotton and silk to weave a variety of items such as fabrics, saris, and dhotis. These fabrics are known for their intricate designs and vibrant colors and are an important part of the traditional attire in many villages.

Agriculture is the backbone of the economy of Indian villages. Many villagers are engaged in farming and agriculture, and it is an important occupation that provides a livelihood for a large portion of the village population. Villagers are known for their traditional farming methods that are in harmony with nature. Agriculture is not only a source of livelihood but also an integral part of the cultural heritage of Indian villages.

Other traditional art forms, crafts and occupations that are practiced in Indian villages include blacksmithing, wood carving, jewelry making and many more. These crafts and occupations not only provide a livelihood for the villagers but also play a significant role in preserving the traditional way of life and customs of the Indian people.

The traditions of Indian villages are an important aspect of the country's cultural heritage. These traditional art forms, crafts, and occupations have been passed down through generations and are an integral part of village life. Pottery, weaving, and agriculture are just a few examples of the traditional art forms, crafts, and occupations that are widely practiced in Indian villages. This chapter will delve deeper into these traditional art forms, crafts and occupations.

☙

"The village is the soul of Indian culture" -
R.K. Narayan

IV

The Architecture of Indian Villages

The Architecture of Indian Villages: An examination of the traditional architectural styles of Indian villages, including the use of mud, bamboo, and other natural materials.

The architecture of Indian villages is a reflection of the country's rich cultural heritage and traditional way of life. The traditional architectural styles of Indian villages are known for their simplicity and practicality, and for the use of locally sourced materials such as mud, bamboo, and other natural materials.

One of the most common traditional architectural styles of Indian villages is the use of mud as a building material. Mud houses are an important part of the traditional architecture of Indian villages. These houses are made by mixing mud and cow dung, and are known for their durability and thermal insulation properties. They are also relatively inexpensive to construct and are well-suited to the local climate and environment.

Bamboo is another traditional building material that is widely used in Indian villages. Bamboo is known for its strength, durability, and flexibility. It is used to construct a variety of buildings in Indian villages, including homes, schools, and community centers. Bamboo houses are also cheaper to construct as compared to other houses and are environmentally friendly.

Other traditional building materials that are commonly used in Indian villages include stone, wood, and thatch. These materials are locally sourced and are well-suited to the local climate and environment.

The architecture of Indian villages is a reflection of the country's rich cultural heritage and traditional way of life. The traditional architectural styles of Indian villages are known for their simplicity and practicality, and for the use of locally sourced materials such as mud, bamboo, and other natural materials. Mud, bamboo, stone, wood, and thatch are some examples of the traditional building materials that are commonly used in Indian villages. This chapter will delve deeper into the traditional architectural styles of Indian villages, including the use of locally sourced materials and the significance of these styles in the daily lives of the villagers.

*"A village is not just a place, it's a way of life" -
Vikas Khanna*

V

The Food and Cuisine of Indian Villages

The Food and Cuisine of Indian Villages: An exploration of the traditional food and cuisine of Indian villages, including the use of locally sourced ingredients and cooking techniques.

The food and cuisine of Indian villages is an important aspect of the country's cultural heritage and reflects the traditional way of life and dietary habits of the villagers. The traditional food and cuisine of Indian villages is characterized by the use of locally sourced ingredients and traditional cooking techniques.

One of the defining features of the food and cuisine of Indian villages is the use of locally sourced ingredients. Villagers rely on locally grown crops such as rice, wheat, and lentils as staple foods. They also use locally available vegetables, fruits, and herbs to prepare a variety of dishes. They also consume locally produced dairy products and meat.

Another defining feature of the food and cuisine of Indian villages is the use of traditional cooking techniques. Villagers use clay ovens, or chulhas, to cook their food. These ovens are made of mud and are fired by burning cow dung cakes. They are known for the unique flavor and taste that they impart to the food. Villagers also use traditional utensils such as earthen pots and iron kadhai to cook their food.

The traditional food and cuisine of Indian villages also reflect the dietary habits of the villagers. Many villages are primarily vegetarian, and the food is mostly based on grains, legumes, and vegetables. Villages that are non-vegetarian, meat is consumed in smaller quantities and mostly in the form of poultry or fish.

The food and cuisine of Indian villages is an important aspect of the country's cultural heritage and reflects the traditional way of life and dietary habits of the villagers. The traditional food and cuisine of Indian villages is characterized by the use of locally sourced ingredients and traditional cooking techniques, and reflects the dietary habits of the villagers. This chapter will delve deeper into the traditional food and cuisine of Indian villages, exploring the various dishes, ingredients, and cooking techniques that are used to prepare them. It will also examine the role of food and cuisine in the cultural heritage of Indian villages and its significance in the daily lives of the villagers. From traditional breakfast dishes like dosa, idli, and puri to the various curries and dals that are prepared using locally sourced ingredients and traditional cooking methods, this chapter aims to provide a comprehensive understanding of the traditional food and cuisine of Indian villages.

"The village is the backbone of India" - B.R. Ambedkar

VI

The Education System of Indian Villages

The Education System of Indian Villages: An examination of the traditional education system of Indian villages and the challenges facing rural communities in terms of access to education.

The education system of Indian villages has traditionally been based on the traditional gurukul system, where children would live with a guru or teacher and receive education in various subjects such as mathematics, science, language, and religious studies. However, this traditional system has been replaced by the modern schooling system in most villages, yet many rural areas still lack access to quality education.

One of the major challenges facing the education system

in Indian villages is the lack of access to schools. Many villages do not have schools or the schools that exist may be of poor quality. This makes it difficult for children to receive an education and limits their future opportunities. Even if the schools are present, the quality of education is often poor due to the lack of qualified teachers, inadequate infrastructure, and a shortage of educational materials.

Another challenge facing the education system in Indian villages is the lack of awareness about the importance of education among parents and the community. Many parents in rural areas do not see the value of education and do not prioritize it for their children. This can lead to low enrollment rates and high dropout rates among school-aged children.

In addition, the traditional system of education has been replaced by the modern schooling system in most villages, but many rural areas still lack access to quality education, and the gap between rural and urban education continues to persist.

Despite these challenges, the government of India has implemented several schemes and programs to improve access to education in rural areas. These include the Sarva Shiksha Abhiyan, which aims to provide universal access to education and the Right to Education Act, which makes education a fundamental right for all children aged 6 to 14.

The education system of Indian villages has traditionally been based on the traditional gurukul system, yet many rural areas still lack access to quality education. The major challenges facing the education system in Indian villages include the lack of access to schools, poor quality of education, lack of awareness about the importance of education and the gap between rural and urban education. Despite these challenges, the government has implemented several schemes and programs to improve access to education in rural areas.

"The village is the essence of India" -
Jawaharlal Nehru

VII

The Health System of Indian Villages

The Health System of Indian Villages: An exploration of the traditional health system of Indian villages and the challenges facing rural communities in terms of access to healthcare.

The health system of Indian villages has traditionally been based on the use of traditional medicine and practices, such as Ayurveda and homeopathy. However, many villages still lack access to modern healthcare facilities and services.

One of the major challenges facing the health system in Indian villages is the lack of access to healthcare facilities and services. Many villages do not have hospitals or health clinics, and those that do may not have the necessary equipment or qualified staff to provide adequate care. This makes it difficult for villagers to receive timely and appropriate medical treatment.

Another challenge facing the health system in Indian villages is the lack of awareness about the importance of healthcare among the villagers. Many villagers in rural areas do not see the value of modern healthcare and prefer to rely on traditional medicine and practices. This can lead to a delay in seeking medical treatment and can also lead to a lack of trust in the modern healthcare system.

Additionally, the shortage of healthcare professionals and the lack of infrastructure in many rural areas, make it difficult for people to access quality healthcare services.

Despite these challenges, the government of India has implemented several schemes and programs to improve access to healthcare in rural areas. These include the National Rural Health Mission, which aims to provide accessible, affordable, and quality healthcare to the rural population, and the Ayushman Bharat scheme, which provides health insurance coverage to the rural poor.

The health system of Indian villages has traditionally been based on the use of traditional medicine and practices, however, many villages still lack access to modern healthcare facilities and services. The major challenges facing the health system in Indian villages include the lack of access to healthcare facilities and services, lack of awareness about the importance of healthcare, shortage of healthcare professionals and lack of infrastructure in many rural areas. Despite these challenges, the government has implemented several schemes and programs to improve access to healthcare in rural areas, with the aim of providing accessible, affordable and quality healthcare to the rural population.

ಲ

"The village is the foundation of Indian civilisation" - Swami Vivekananda

VIII

The Role of Women in Indian Villages

The Role of Women in Indian Villages: An examination of the traditional roles and responsibilities of women in Indian villages and the challenges they face in modern society.

The role of women in Indian villages is an important aspect of the country's cultural heritage and reflects the traditional way of life and societal norms of the villagers. Historically, the traditional roles and responsibilities of women in Indian villages have been primarily domestic, such as taking care of the household, raising children, and working in the fields. However, women in modern society are facing many challenges as they try to navigate their traditional roles and new opportunities.

One of the major challenges facing women in Indian villages is the lack of access to education and employment opportunities. Many women in rural areas do not have the opportunity to receive an education and are therefore limited in terms of the employment opportunities that are available to them. This can lead to a lack of economic independence and increased vulnerability to poverty and domestic violence.

Another challenge facing women in Indian villages is the societal expectation that they will prioritize their family and domestic responsibilities over their own personal and professional development. This can lead to a lack of autonomy and decision-making power, and can also limit their ability to access healthcare and other services.

Additionally, gender-based discrimination and violence are also prevalent in Indian villages, and women often face discrimination in terms of access to resources and opportunities, and they may also be subject to physical and emotional abuse.

Despite these challenges, there are efforts being made to empower women in Indian villages. The government has implemented several schemes and programs aimed at empowering women, such as the Pradhan Mantri Ujjwala Yojana, which aims to provide LPG connections to women from below poverty line households, and the Beti Bachao Beti Padhao campaign, which aims to improve the welfare and education of the girl child.

The role of women in Indian villages is an important aspect of the country's cultural heritage and reflects the traditional way of life and societal norms of the villagers. However, women in modern society are facing many challenges as they try to navigate their traditional roles and new opportunities, such as lack of access to education and employment opportunities, societal expectations, discrimination and violence. Despite these challenges, there are efforts being made to empower women in Indian villages through government schemes and programs, as well as through grassroots initiatives aimed at promoting education, healthcare, and economic independence among women in rural areas. This chapter will delve deeper into the traditional roles and responsibilities of women in Indian villages, as well as the challenges they face in modern society and the efforts being made to empower them. It will also examine the impact of these changes on the cultural heritage of Indian villages and on the daily lives of the villagers.

*"The village is the heart of India" -
Rabindranath Tagore*

IX

The Role of Men in Indian Villages

The Role of Men in Indian Villages: An examination of the traditional roles and responsibilities of men in Indian villages and the challenges they face in modern society.

The role of women in Indian villages is an important aspect of the country's cultural heritage and reflects the traditional way of life and societal norms of the villagers. Historically, the traditional roles and responsibilities of women in Indian villages have been primarily domestic, such as taking care of the household, raising children, and working in the fields. However, women in modern society are facing many challenges as they try to navigate their traditional roles and new opportunities.

One of the major challenges facing women in Indian villages is the lack of access to education and employment opportunities. Many women in rural areas do not have the opportunity to receive an education and are therefore limited in terms of the employment opportunities that are available to them. This can lead to a lack of economic independence and increased vulnerability to poverty and domestic violence.

Another challenge facing women in Indian villages is the societal expectation that they will prioritize their family and domestic responsibilities over their own personal and professional development. This can lead to a lack of autonomy and decision-making power, and can also limit their ability to access healthcare and other services.

Additionally, gender-based discrimination and violence are also prevalent in Indian villages, and women often face discrimination in terms of access to resources and opportunities, and they may also be subject to physical and emotional abuse.

Despite these challenges, there are efforts being made to empower women in Indian villages. The government has implemented several schemes and programs aimed at empowering women, such as the Pradhan Mantri Ujjwala Yojana, which aims to provide LPG connections to women from below poverty line households, and the Beti Bachao Beti Padhao campaign, which aims to improve the welfare and education of the girl child.

The role of women in Indian villages is an important aspect of the country's cultural heritage and reflects the traditional way of life and societal norms of the villagers. However, women in modern society are facing many challenges as they try to navigate their traditional roles and new opportunities, such as lack of access to education and employment opportunities, societal expectations, discrimination and violence. Despite these challenges, there are efforts being made to empower women in Indian villages through government schemes and programs, as well as through grassroots initiatives aimed at promoting education, healthcare, and economic independence among women in rural areas.

This chapter will delve deeper into the traditional roles and responsibilities of women in Indian villages, as well as the challenges they face in modern society and the efforts being made to empower them. It will also examine the impact of these changes on the cultural heritage of Indian villages and on the daily lives of the villagers.

"The village is the pulse of India" - A.P.J. Abdul Kalam

X

The Challenges Facing Indian Villages

The Challenges Facing Indian Villages: An exploration of the challenges facing Indian villages in modern times, including poverty, lack of access to education and healthcare, and environmental degradation.

The challenges facing Indian villages in modern times are complex and varied, and they pose a significant threat to the country's cultural heritage and the well-being of its rural population. Some of the major challenges include poverty, lack of access to education and healthcare, and environmental degradation.

One of the major challenges facing Indian villages is poverty. Many rural areas are characterized by low levels of income and high levels of unemployment. This can lead to a lack of access to basic necessities such as food, shelter, and healthcare, and can also limit opportunities for education and economic advancement.

Another challenge facing Indian villages is the lack of access to education and healthcare. Many villages do not have schools or healthcare facilities, and those that do may not have the necessary equipment or qualified staff to provide adequate care. This can lead to a lack of opportunities for personal and professional development, and can also limit the ability of villagers to access essential services.

Environmental degradation is also a significant challenge facing Indian villages. Many rural areas are characterized by poor air and water quality, as well as deforestation and land degradation. These issues can have a negative impact on the health and livelihoods of villagers and also on the cultural heritage of Indian villages.

Despite these challenges, there are efforts being made to address these issues and improve the lives of people living in Indian villages. The government has implemented several schemes and programs aimed at reducing poverty, improving access to education and healthcare, and protecting the environment.

The challenges facing Indian villages in modern times are complex and varied, and they pose a significant threat to the country's cultural heritage and the well-being of its rural population. Major challenges include poverty, lack of access to education and healthcare, and environmental degradation. Despite these challenges, there are efforts being made to address these issues and improve the lives of people living in Indian villages.

"A village is a refuge for so many philosphers." – Arthur Symons

XI

The Future of Indian Villages

The Future of Indian Villages: An examination of the efforts being made to preserve and promote the culture, traditions, and way of life of Indian villages, and the potential for sustainable development in rural communities.

The future of Indian villages is a topic of great importance, as it has a direct impact on the cultural heritage of the country and the well-being of its rural population. There are various efforts being made to preserve and promote the culture, traditions, and way of life of Indian villages, and also to promote sustainable development in rural communities.

One of the main efforts being made to preserve the culture and traditions of Indian villages is through the promotion of traditional art forms, crafts, and occupations. This includes initiatives to revive traditional crafts such as pottery, weaving, and agriculture, as well as efforts to promote traditional art forms such as folk music, dance, and festivals. This helps to keep these traditional practices alive and also provides economic opportunities for villagers.

Another effort being made to preserve the culture of Indian villages is through the promotion of sustainable development. This includes initiatives to promote sustainable agriculture and renewable energy, as well as efforts to conserve the environment and protect natural resources. These efforts not only help to preserve the culture of Indian villages, but they also contribute to the overall well-being of the rural population by providing economic opportunities and improving access to basic necessities such as food and water.

Additionally, there are also efforts to promote education and healthcare in rural communities, to improve the standard of living for the villagers.

The future of Indian villages is a topic of great importance, as it has a direct impact on the cultural heritage of the country and the well-being of its rural population. There are various efforts being made to preserve and promote the culture, traditions, and way of life of Indian villages, and also to promote sustainable development in rural communities. These efforts include the promotion of traditional art forms, crafts, and occupations, sustainable development, and education and healthcare.

ಌ

Other Books Of The Author

1. The Moments When I Met God
2. Kashiyile Theertha Pathangal
3. GURU GYAN VANI
4. Abhiprerak Gita
5. ASSI SE JAIN GHAT TAK
6. Hopelessness of Arjuna
7. The Soul and It's True Nature
8. Sense of Action (Karma)
9. Action through Wisdom
10. Action through Wisdom
11. THEORY AND PRACTICAL OF EVERY ACTION
12. LOGICAL UNDERSTANDING OF THE SUPREME
13. THE IMPERISHABLE SUPREME
14. Yatra Nishadraj se Hanuman Ghat Tak
15. Yatra Karnatak Ghat se Raja Ghat Tak
16. Yatra Pandey Ghat se Prayagraj Ghat Tak
17. Yatra Ranjendra Prasad Ghat se Dattatreya Ghat Tak
18. YaatraSindhiya Ghat se Gwaliar Ghat Tak
19. Yatra Mangala Gauri Ghat se Hanuman Gadhi Ghat Tak
20. Yatra Gaay Ghat Se Nishad Ghat Tak
21. MAA GANGA, GHATEN EVM UTSAV
22. Ganga Arti Dev Deepavali evam Any Utsav
23. Potentials of Digitalized India
24. VEDIC CONSCIOUSNESS
25. A Brief Introduction to Vedic Science
26. Kashi ke Barah Jyotirling
27. IMPACT OF MOTIVATION
28. Let's have a Milky Way Journey
29. Color Therapy in a Nutshell

30. Rigveda in a Nutshell
31. Yajurveda in a Nutshell
32. Samveda in a Nutshell
33. Atharva Veda in a Nutshell
34. Ayushman Bhava - Ayurveda
35. Srimad Bhagavad Gita and Upanishad Connection
36. Srimad Bhagavad Gita - an attempt to summarize each chapter.
37. Facts and Impact of Nakshatra
38. Astro Gems - NAVARATNA
39. Ekadashi - A Concise Overview
40. A Concise View of Hanuman Chalisa
41. Inspirational Gita
42. Nakshatraranyam
43. Summary of 18 Mahapuranas
44. Synopsis of 18 Upa Puranas
45. Rigvediya Upanishads
46. Shukla Yajurvediya Upanishads
47. Krishna Yajurvediya Upanishads
48. Samavediya Upanishads
49. Atharvavediya Upanishads
50. The Seven Great Sages
51. From Rocket Scientist to President Dr. APJ Abdul Kalam
52. The Visionary's Voice - Quotes of Dr. APJ Abdul Kalam
53. The Wisdom of Swami Vivekananda: Insights and Inspiration from a Legendary Spiritual Teacher
54. Ayurvedic Remedies from the Garden
55. Sages and Seers
56. Rising Strong – Motivational Stories of Women
57. Beyond Flames -Mystery stories of Funeral Ghat Manikarnika
58. The Origins of Tulsi: A Look at the Mythological Roots of the Plant"

ૹ

CONTACT

DR. JAGADEESH PILLAI

PhD in Vedic Science

Four Times Guinness World Record Holder

Winner of Mahatma Gandhi Vishwa Shanti Puraskar and
Global Peace Ambassador

Gemology, Astro & Vastu Consultant - Spiritual Counselor

Consultant for designing World Record Ideas

Efficient Tarot Card Reader

9839093003

myrichindia@gmail.com

drjagadeeshpillai@facebook

drjagadeeshpillai@instagram

jagadeeshpillai@youtube

www. JAGADEESHPILLAI.com

|| LOKAHA SAMASTHAHA SUKHINO BHAVANTU ||

• 65 •